D0609539

CALGARY PUBLIC LIBRARY

DISCARD
FISH CREEK
AREA LIBRARY

j 940. 5373 WIN
Windrow, Martin.
World War II GI.
95532030

CALGARY PUBLIC LIBRARY

FISH CREEK
AREA LIBRARY

THE SOLDIER THROUGH THE AGES

THE WORLD WAR 11
G1

Martin Windrow

Illustrated by
Kevin Lyles

DISCARD

Franklin Watts
London   New York   Toronto   Sydney

© Franklin Watts Ltd 1986

First published in Great Britain in 1986 by
Franklin Watts Limited
12a Golden Square
London W1

First published in the USA by
Franklin Watts Inc.
387 Park Avenue South
New York
N.Y. 10016

First published in Australia by
Franklin Watts Australia
14 Mars Road
Lane Cove
NSW 2066

UK edition ISBN: 0 86313 300 2
US edition ISBN: 0-531-10084-7
Library of Congress Catalog Card
No: 85-50765

Designed by James Marks

Printed in Belgium

Contents

Total war

Between September 1939 and August 1945 the world was torn apart by World War II – at a cost of some 55 million lives. This global conflict raged across almost all Europe, North Africa, China, Southeast Asia and all the oceans of the world.

In December 1941 the Japanese raid on the US base at Pearl Harbor in Hawaii brought the United States into the war. The United States was the world's richest industrial nation; and there was no doubt about the final Allied victory from that time onward. But the road to victory over the cruel dictatorships of Nazi Germany, Imperial Japan and Fascist Italy was to be long and agonizing. One of the heroes of that bloodstained journey was the American infantryman.

He called himself GI, as if he were just another piece of equipment stamped "government issue." But he was far from being a faceless tool of war. In fact, he was not a professional soldier, but rather a civilian in uniform.

▷ A typical GI, in the ruined landscape of Europe, winter 1944–5. The US Army was well equipped with trucks, tanks, artillery and huge supporting air forces, but it was still the infantry who bore the worst of the war. Only infantrymen can actually occupy and hold the ground from which the enemy has been driven by machines and explosives. Battle casualties caused a real shortage of infantry late in the war; units had to stay in the front line for far too long at a time.

The young American GI served for the duration of the war, fighting far from home. In Europe he was sent against campaign-hardened soldiers of the German Army who had been fighting, and usually winning, for the previous three years. In the jungles and on the coral islands of the Pacific he faced Japanese troops of skill and courage. Yet, in the end, the GI won because he learned to be as good a soldier as his enemies.

The GIs had to have high morale to sustain themselves in the face of frightening danger and wretched discomfort. Certainly, they loved their country, hated tyranny, and respected the men who led them in battle. But most important was a feeling of responsibility toward their comrades – the few men of their own small squad. They felt that they could not let their friends down. This spirit of comradeship is one of the things that war brings out in ordinary men and women.

No matter how often soldiers went into battle, they never really got used to combat. Although veterans learned what to expect, there seemed to be a limit to the amount of physical and emotional stress a man could absorb. If troops were not pulled out of battle before reaching their breaking point, they suffered a form of nervous exhaustion known as "combat fatigue." The true bravery of the American civilian-in-uniform lay in the fact that he kept going when he was hungry, cold, wet, asleep on his feet and unashamedly scared.

The ruthless and unrestrained use of powerful weapons made this a "total war." Cities were bombed to rubble; passenger ships were sunk without warning; civilians were killed in huge numbers. But the GI tried to treat the helpless civilians as decently as he could, and most of the war-torn world looked upon the American soldier as a real liberator.

Basic training

The typical GI was in his early twenties. Many GIs volunteered for the Army, but most entered the service through a system of conscription called "the draft."

Training time varied. If a whole new division of about 12,000 men was being formed, training lasted a year (later reduced to 37 weeks). Men being trained to be sent overseas as replacements for casualties in units already fighting only received 26 weeks' training, which was later cut to 13. A serious shortage of infantry in the winter of 1944 saw some recruits on their way after only six weeks.

First, the independent-minded recruit was taught to obey orders swiftly and without argument, and to do everything "the Army way." This was achieved by a lot of loud shouting, some mild bullying and endlessly repeated drills. When he had acquired a cooperative attitude, he was shown the equipment and taught the skills of soldiering. Gradually his confidence was built up again so that he took pride in his new abilities and his new identity. He no longer thought of himself as "John Smith, individual," but as "Private Smith, 26th Infantry, US Army." It was a rough process, but it was necessary. The recruits would soon face much worse challenges than harsh drill sergeants, so they *had* to be able to act together, quickly.

△ Building up physical fitness was a vital part of basic training.

▽ Recruits were taught how to shoot – and handle guns safely – on the range.

◁ "Battle training" meant pounding around obstacle courses and crawling under barbed wire, while instructors threw smoke bombs, and live machine guns fired over the recruits' heads. Training helped accustom raw recruits to the sounds of battle, but it could only partially prepare them for the real thing. Much of what they learned had to be "unlearned" when they reached the front – the only real battle school.

Overseas

When World War II broke out in Europe in 1939, the US Army had just 200,000 men. Its five combat divisions – battle groups of infantry, tank and artillery units mixed in various ways, each about 12,000 strong – were mainly organized for home defense. But once America joined the Allied cause in December 1941, her war effort soon outstripped that of any other country except Russia. In 1943, the busiest year, two and a half million recruits went into the service. By 1945 the Army had over eight million men and women in uniform and had sent no fewer than 89 divisions to war. Nearly five million GIs served overseas, and of every hundred men, four were killed and nearly 13 were wounded.

For the infantry, the war was more dangerous than those figures suggest.

Because this complex modern army had so many special types of technical, supply and administrative units, only 38 of every hundred sent overseas were combat soldiers – but these men suffered three-quarters of the losses. So of the actual fighting soldiers, one in three was killed or wounded. This huge increase in the number of "rear area" troops was something new in history; it was calculated that in the Pacific it took 18 "rear area" soldiers to keep one man fighting in the front line. Although their jobs were essential, these soldiers were naturally not popular with the men who took the real risks.

In one way overseas service was a great adventure. In the 1930s foreign travel was unusual, and very few of the boys who found themselves in uniform had ever traveled far from their hometowns. Now they were shipped all over the world – to Britain and later to France, Belgium and Germany; to North Africa, Sicily and Italy; to Australia, the Pacific islands, China and eventually to Japan.

Because distances were so great, home leave during the war was almost unknown. Many GIs were away from their families for nearly four years without a break and got very homesick. Regular letters from home were important to keep their spirits up, and the services made great efforts to deliver mail reliably.

◁ A GI gets his first look at a British port scarred by bombing. Air raids killed some 50,000 British men, women and children by early 1942.

Uniforms and harness

Nowadays all soldiers have two types of uniforms: a formal one for parades and furlough, and a harder-wearing set of clothes for actual combat. The US Army was the first to adopt this sensible system. Just before World War II the GI was issued with a field jacket, made like a civilian windbreaker. Replaced in 1943 by other, improved types, it was still an important step forward, later copied by most other armies.

Colorful badges and shoulder patches were worn on the dress uniforms which were no longer exposed to battle. They identified branch of service, division, regiment, rank and various skill qualifications, as well as awards for gallantry and participation in various campaigns. From 1944 the favorite out-of-battle uniform was the "Ike" jacket, nicknamed after the American commander of all Allied troops in Europe, General Dwight D. Eisenhower.

The GI's helmet came in two parts. The strap and headband were fixed to a light inner liner, with a separate steel outer shell. In emergencies the shell could be used for digging, carrying water and for many other chores.

The well-designed battle harness of tough woven cotton webbing accommodated the GI's clothing, ammunition, first-aid supplies, rations and mess kit, entrenching tool, blankets, waterproof poncho, etc.

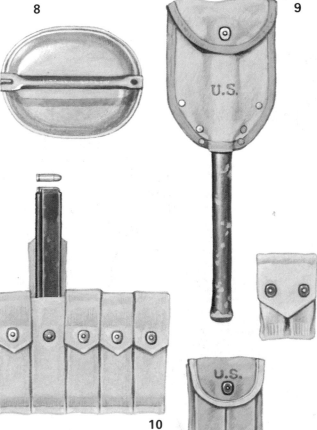

◁ **1** The two-part M1 helmet.
2 The 1941 field jacket.
3 No longer worn in battle, the 1944 "Ike" uniform jacket could display many kinds of colorful insignia: *collar*, US and infantry branch discs; *left arm*, 1st Infantry Division patch, above rank chevrons (corporal), above two 6-month overseas service stripes; *left chest*, Combat Infantryman badge marking actual battle service, above ribbons of Bronze Star medal for gallantry, and Europe/Africa/Middle East Campaign medal.
4 Garrison cap; pale blue piping for infantry, and regimental crest – here, 26th Infantry.

△ **5** Web belt with "suspenders" had 10 rifle clip pouches and first-aid packet – extra dressings and grenades were sometimes taped on too.
6 Two-part pack, attached to suspenders, held clothes, personal items and rations. Bayonet and entrenching spade could be clipped to pack, and coats, blankets etc. could be fixed round edges.
7 Canteen, fitted inside a cup, carried in belt pouch.
8 Pair of mess tins.
9 Folding entrenching spade.
10 Different guns needed different ammunition pouches on the belt: long ones for "Tommy gun" magazines, shorter ones for carbine and pistol.

Allies

Most GIs who fought in Europe were first sent to Great Britain. In 1942 they arrived on ocean liners and transports at the rate of 20,000 a week. Before this time, not many ordinary Britons and Americans knew much about one another's way of life. The next three years would bring them closer together than ever before. The feelings of shared danger in wartime created a special bond. This friendship has strengthened right up to the present day, and there is still an ongoing sense of goodwill between the two nations.

Some GIs were based in training camps in Britain for two years before they were sent across the English Channel to fight in France. Many got to know British families and were invited into British homes. There American soldiers saw an unfamiliar way of life.

An American solider in Britain was paid almost four times more than his British army equivalent. Some US Army sergeants earned more than British captains. This led to some lively encounters in British pubs, where British Tommies felt that more highly paid GIs could take their girlfriends away from them.

Food rationing for British civilians was very strict: one person per week lived on such small amounts as 4 ounces of bacon, 2 ounces of tea, one ounce of cheese, and a tiny meat ration. This was usually Spam mixed with a strange concoction of carrots, potatoes, and turnips. Similar rationing in the States existed and was known by most of the GIs, but it was somewhat more generous.

To help explain the differences in life, the US Army gave each GI a booklet that explained British customs. This helpful advice covered serious matters, such as the point that Britain had been fighting this war since 1939. But it also touched more light-hearted areas, such as the fact that certain slang words, harmless in the USA, meant more unfortunate things to the British!

▷ Men of many armies were fighting together for the Allied cause, and GIs had a bewildering variety of badges and shoulder patches to learn to recognize. These examples are: **1** Scottish Seaforth Highlander; **2** Free French naval infantryman; **3** Polish 10th Hussars tank crewman; **4** Queen's Own Rifles of Canada; **5** British Inns of Court Regt. armored car officer.

▽ A GI visits his British girlfriend's home. Like one in every five British adults at that time, she is a member of the uniformed services.

The real thing

After their long preparation, the GIs destined to liberate northern Europe with their allies finally stormed ashore on the Normandy beaches on June 6, 1944: "D-Day." Before dawn nearly 6,500 transport ships, 4,000 landing barges and 200 warships took about 200,000 US, British, Canadian and other Allied soldiers, sailors and marines across the English Channel. Above them, 24,000 paratroopers and glider troops flew through the dark sky. By nightfall on D-Day, 145,000 of them were on French soil – and 55,000 of those were GIs. On that first day 4,650 Americans were killed or wounded.

Enemy resistance was only moderate on the beach code-named "Utah," where 23,000 GIs got ashore with only 197 casualties. But "Omaha" beach was a nightmare: many GIs of the 1st and 29th Divisions, after months of training, fell under massive enemy fire without ever seeing an enemy soldier or firing a shot themselves.

Some units were veterans of battles in Tunisia and Sicily; others were inexperienced – but fought well, since they did not know enough about war to be as scared as they should have been. In the eleven months before the final victory in Europe, they would learn a great deal. Few men who landed on D-Day were still alive, unhurt, and with their units at the end of the European war.

Looking back, we may think Allied victory was inevitable; but that was no help to the individual GI. Although two-thirds of the German Army were fighting in Russia, the campaign in the West was as hard for the GIs as any war in history. Losses were high, and tired units were kept in battle for up to a month at a time. Modern weapons and modern tactics made great demands on the GI's courage and endurance.

◁ Heavily loaded GIs scramble down rope nets over the side of a transport ship before jumping awkwardly into the pitching, landing craft which are lined up alongside to take them the last part of the journey to the Normandy beaches. This descent was one of the most frightening things that GIs recalled about D-Day: loaded with at least 70 lb (32 kg) of equipment, a soldier was usually doomed to drown if he slipped. In fact, many GIs did drown on D-Day. Some were in landing craft sunk far from the beach by enemy fire, while others were simply unloaded in water too deep to wade. At the water's edge they faced steel obstacles wired with explosive charges; and, at Omaha beach, a deadly crossfire from enemy gunners in concrete positions which had survived naval and air bombardment. More than 2,000 GIs died in the water or on the narrow beach at Omaha, before a few brave men led the attack inland.

Firepower

▽ **1** Most GIs used the .30 in (7.62 mm) M1 rifle, accurate to 1,200 yd (1,100 m). After loading a tin clip of 8 cartridges, they just kept pulling the trigger, emptying a clip in about 3 seconds. The "self-loading" mechanism threw out the empty cartridge, fed in a new one and cocked the firing mechanism automatically after each shot.

2 Officers often carried the lighter, shorter-range carbine – a more realistic weapon in modern combat than a pistol like the Colt automatic (**3**) which was accurate only to about 27 yd (25 m) at most. Many veteran officers preferred to carry rifles like their men.

The GI carried the most powerful, accurate and fast-firing weapons of any infantryman the world had yet seen. And he was encouraged to use as much ammunition as he needed. It was not only a matter of firing single, aimed shots. With his quick-firing weapons the GI could fill the air with a storm of bullets. If that made an enemy duck for cover, giving the GI the chance to run to the next place of shelter, then it was

ammunition well spent even if it hit nobody.

At any date from about 1680 to about 1880, a squad of ten foot soldiers of any army could fire only about 30 shots in a minute. Ten GIs of World War II could fire about 2,300 shots a minute from their rifles, sub-machine guns and Browning Automatic Rifles – and with much greater accuracy.

◁ Two to four men in each ten-man squad had guns which fired in bursts, like machine guns. The M3 "Grease gun" (4) – so called from its shape – and the Browning Automatic Rifle (5) each held 20 shots, firing up to 500 a minute. The M3 was accurate only to about 110 yd (100 m); the longer-barreled BAR, to 650 yd (600 m).

△ GIs also used hand grenades: small, powerful bombs light enough to be thrown a good distance. The soldier pulled out a pin securing the fuse lever while holding the lever down with his fingers. When he threw the grenade, the lever sprang off, starting a 4-second time fuse; then he had to duck quickly to avoid the flying steel splinters.

A deadly game of leapfrog

The great firepower of modern weapons made the old-fashioned, massed frontal attack suicidally dangerous. World War II infantry attacked by "fire and movement." Fairly small groups leapfrogged forward, one group firing while the other rushed for the next bit of cover. The smallest "building-block" of combat was a section of about 10 men, including at least one machine gun; even the single section could make a leapfrog advance, with the riflemen and machine-gun team moving alternately. Much larger units could use the same basic tactics, with whole companies alternating, and the battalion's heavy weapons company giving supporting fire. Tanks were mixed with infantry to support the GIs. The classic attack went in from several directions to split the defenders' fire.

A GI in Europe in 1944–5 might have to make about 35 different attacks over his eleven months' fighting. Since the Allies were attacking to liberate previously lost ground, they always faced defenders who had had time to build dangerous positions. Deep, interlocking lines of bunkers, machine-gun and artillery positions, dug-in tanks and infantry trenches were linked to natural obstacles – rivers, woods and hills – over many miles.

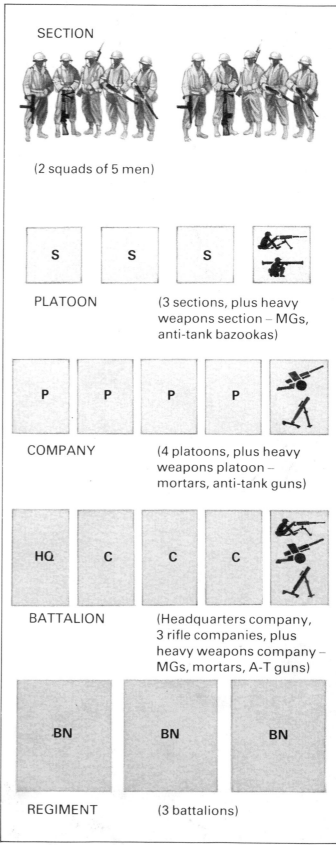

SECTION

(2 squads of 5 men)

PLATOON

| S | S | S | [heavy weapons] |

(3 sections, plus heavy weapons section – MGs, anti-tank bazookas)

COMPANY

| P | P | P | P | [heavy weapons] |

(4 platoons, plus heavy weapons platoon – mortars, anti-tank guns)

BATTALION

| HQ | C | C | C | [heavy weapons] |

(Headquarters company, 3 rifle companies, plus heavy weapons company – MGs, mortars, A-T guns)

REGIMENT

| BN | BN | BN |

(3 battalions)

△ Typical attack on enemy defending houses:

1 US transport left in rear.
2 US mortars open fire from one flank.
3 US tanks advance in a flanking attack.
4 On other flank US infantry machine gunners open fire after working forward along hedges.
5 US infantry advance in short rushes, while mortars, tanks, MGs "keep enemy heads down" and split their defensive fire among the different groups.

▷ Makeup of a US infantry regiment; three regiments, with supporting units of special troops – signals, engineers, artillery, etc. – formed a division. In theory there were 5 officers and about 190 men per company; 36 officers and 800 men per battalion. Losses often reduced the figures greatly. A 19-year-old replacement could find himself promoted platoon sergeant within a month of his first experience of battle, leading 30 other men.

19

Mortars, machine guns and mines

The GI was equipped with – and had to face – a whole new class of heavy weapons unknown before the closing stages of World War I. These mortars and machine guns were essential to the new "fire and movement" tactics. By World War II they were light enough to be carried by two or three men, but powerful enough to give the infantry platoon the means to shoot their way through quite serious opposition without outside help. Every section had one machine gun; every platoon had a few mortars; and special "heavy weapons" units in each battalion had more of them to fire in support of the rifle companies. (Of course, since the enemy had them too, the advantages more or less cancelled out.)

Machine guns were much lighter, handier and faster-firing than their World War I equivalents. Mortars lobbed powerful bombs over any range from a few dozen paces to about 2,500 yd ($2\frac{1}{2}$ km). The bomb fired automatically when it was dropped down the tube, and a good crew could have 10 in the air at once. A three-tube mortar platoon might fire 1,000 bombs in a couple of hours in battle. The GI particularly hated the German six-barrel "Moaning Minnie" mortar, whose bombs made a ghastly howling noise in the air.

▽ Each German infantry section had a .30 in (7.92 mm) belt-fed light machine gun like this MG 34 type. It fired 800 rounds a minute, accurate to 800 yd (730 m).

◁ Standard German World War II $3\frac{1}{2}$ in (81 mm) mortar, firing $7\frac{3}{4}$ lb ($3\frac{1}{2}$ kg) bombs. The mortar came apart into carrying loads for three soldiers, while a fourth carried ammunition.

◁ The dreaded German S-mine jumped into the air when stepped on, exploding at chest height and spraying deadly steel balls in all directions. To be caught in a minefield was a terrifying experience.
Below German anti-tank Tellermine 42.

Another new weapon particularly feared by all foot soldiers was the land mine – the buried bomb, which blew up when you stepped on it. Millions were laid on the battlefields of World War II; they were a cheap, easy way for defenders to cover the approaches to their positions. In the battle of the Hürtgen Forest in Germany in the winter of 1944–5, it was found that one forest track concealed one mine every eight paces for 3 miles (5 km).

Among World War II GIs, bullets were responsible for only one in every four men killed or wounded. The rest fell victim to artillery, mortars, mines and grenades. Most men never even saw or heard the enemy soldier who killed or wounded them.

▽ Mines could be spotted and made safe if the GI had time for a patient search – which was not often the case in battle. By late in the war electronic metal detectors were being issued, but there were seldom enough to go around. Most GIs had to search the hard way – by prodding the ground with a bayonet, step by step.

Life in a hole in the ground

The European campaign of 1944–5 took the GI from the Normandy beaches to central Germany in just 11 months. Compared with the long stalemate of World War I, this was a war of movement. But although the Allies had huge numbers of trucks and tanks, in fact the infantry still spent most of its time burrowing underground.

The war of movement came to a halt every time the GIs ran into enemy opposition, which was most days. Fighting was done on foot, in short rushes followed by pauses. The enemy counter-attacked as soon as they lost any ground, so the advancing GIs had to "dig in" to defend what they had just captured.

If the GI stopped in one place for longer than an hour or two, he had to dig himself a one-man "foxhole" or two-man slit trench for protection against the inevitable barrage of artillery shells. Digging a hole about 4 ft deep, 6 ft long and 3 ft across (1.2 m by 1.8 m by .9 m) is extremely hard work; and the GI's life depended on doing this back-breaking chore, at top speed, several times each week. And when he had dug it, he had to live in it . . .

Autumn 1944 was very rainy, and the winter of 1944–5 the coldest for 38 years. Living and sleeping in freezing mud, the GI had no chance to dry or warm himself for days or even weeks on end. Since combat troops never got more than three or four hours' sleep a night, it is hardly surprising that these cold, wet, filthy, exhausted men often fell ill. In January 1945 100 men a day from the 30th Division were falling ill simply from the effects of living in the open – equivalent to a whole battalion a week, before counting actual battle casualties.

△ A group of GIs in a Normandy orchard make the most of their brief rest in the sun: from August 19, 1944 onward, it hardly ever stopped raining in France! While an NCO distributes letters from home, men improve their "foxholes" or heat up their field rations on little bottled-gas stoves. Ration packs held enough for three mixed meals a day. Most food was dried or canned: fruit or cereal bars, crackers, various canned meat-and-vegetable mixtures, candy and coffee powder were included. (Packs also contained cigarettes, chewing gum and toilet paper.) In battle, GIs had few chances to heat food properly. Rations were not designed to support men fighting in bad weather for weeks on end, especially when eaten cold; they lacked bulk and proper vitamins.

War in the Pacific

Japan's surprise attack on the US fleet at Pearl Harbor on December 7, 1941 was the event that brought America into World War II on the side of the Allies. From then until August 1945, US and Japanese soldiers, marines, sailors and airmen fought a savage campaign among the islands scattered across the vast Pacific Ocean. In many ways the Pacific War was a harsher ordeal for the GI than the campaigns in Europe.

The climate of most battlefields was unhealthy and exhausting, especially to tense, overtired soldiers. In the wet season, tropical rains of more than 10 in (25 cm) a day were recorded. In the constant, stifling, muggy heat of the jungle soldiers found their skin turning white and puckering into wrinkles, as if they had lain too long in a bath. Every little cut or sore festered, and skin diseases were very common. Among the many dangerous insects were mosquitoes which spread malaria – it was calculated that one out of every two men who served in the Pacific caught this disease. Exhaustion and illness could cause healthy young men to lose as much as 45 lb (20 kg) in a few weeks.

The jungle was not only hot and damp; it was dark, tangled, evil-smelling – and very frightening. In the gloom under the trees GIs could not see clearly for more than a few paces. Their enemy was a brilliant jungle fighter, skilled at concealment: at any moment he might open fire from some nearby but overlooked hiding place, dug into the ground and covered

▷ US Marines in combat uniforms printed with jungle camouflage fight their way inland after landing on a Japanese-held Pacific island. One Marine gives water to a wounded comrade; in the background, smoke rises from enemy positions attacked by US aircraft and shelled by ships off shore.

These men will soon have to clear the enemy-defended jungle step by step. The Japanese were masters of fortification and camouflage. They defended strong, well-hidden bunkers to the death; and the Marines and GIs needed all the support they could get from planes and navy gunfire. Island battles were fairly brief, but very savage and costly.

with heavy logs. The Japanese were fanatically brave and would rather fight to the death than surrender: on one island only 17 out of 5,000 were taken alive.

Because it took a considerable time to make the complex arrangements for each new amphibious landing on an enemy-held island, the GI in the Pacific usually had longer breaks between battles than he did in Europe. But when the landing craft did finally drop him in some shell-churned lagoon, he faced terribly hard fighting. On Tarawa Atoll on November 20, 1943, the 5,000 US assault troops suffered 1,500 casualties on the first day, capturing a strip of land along the edge of the water which was nowhere more than 250 yd (230 m) wide.

Street fighting

Some of the GI's most dangerous battles were fought in ruined towns, as the Allies advanced across Europe in 1944–5. Though shelled and bombed to rubble, stone and brick buildings offered brave, skillful defenders excellent hiding places for their machine guns, anti-tank rocket launchers, cannons and snipers. Ruins actually gave better protection than undamaged buildings, and rubble-choked streets slowed down the attackers. The GIs had to fight their way from house to house in a deadly game of hide-and-seek. They risked death if they lost their concentration for even a moment.

CITROËN

PHARMACIE

116

CAFE

CAFE

On the poster: TOI AUSSI! TES CAMARADES T'ATTENDENT DANS LA DIVISION FRANÇAISE DE WAFFEN-SS

REVOLUTION NATIONALE

◁ As GIs scramble for cover in the ruins, a Panther tank supports an enemy counterattack. The American officer calls up his bazooka anti-tank rocket launcher. In battle, tanks and foot soldiers had to co-operate. Tanks could destroy machine guns, which menaced the infantry; but tanks were almost "blind," so they needed infantry to fight off bazooka teams.

Morphine, penicillin-and luck

Between 1941 and 1945 more than 640,000 GIs were wounded: this was nearly 13 out of every 100 men who served overseas. The infantry suffered by far the worst. Although they made up only one-fifth of the army's total strength, they bore two-thirds of all the casualties. Luckily for them the American medical services were second to none, both in size and skill. Medicine had made great advances in this period, thanks to new discoveries.

Of every 100 men wounded in the Civil War, nearly 14 died. By 1941–5 only 4.5 per cent died of their wounds. The army had efficient arrangements for getting the wounded off the battlefield and into well-equipped hospitals. There the GI could be treated by techniques unknown in 1918.

Every front-line medic carried morphine to dull the pain of wounds. New drugs, such as penicillin and "sulfa," prevented wounds from becoming infected and saved tens of thousands of lives. New methods of storing blood until it was needed enabled life-saving transfusions to be given. (In World War I transfusions had only been possible directly from one man to another, and donors could not always be found.)

▽ Bandaged and drugged, a wounded GI is left, marked by his upright rifle, for the follow-up medical teams to find. Each GI had a first aid pack of bandages and basic drugs to use on himself or his buddy. Medics went into battle with the soldiers, but could not stay with them long – others needed their help.

Throughout history many more soldiers have died of disease than of wounds. In World War II there were still 27 times more patients suffering from disease or accident than from wounds. But now the new drugs could save them too – 997 out of every 1,000 sick men recovered.

Even when the GI left the army and went home, he was not forgotten. A law called the GI Bill of Rights awarded him generous money grants toward his education and the cost of a home or business. War was far more costly and little less cruel than in ancient times. But at least people now accepted the duty not to abandon their soldiers as soon as the guns fell silent.

▽ If – and it was a big "if" – the stretcher-bearers found him in time, the GI had a far better chance of living than the soldier of any earlier war. Blood transfusions fought the shock of wounds and replaced vital fluid. In 1945, of every four men hit in the stomach, three survived; an incredible 19 of every 20 chest wounds were not fatal; even men with limbs blown off, or head wounds, were saved more often than not.

Glossary

Amphibious warfare Combined land and sea fighting, involving putting troops ashore from ships under fire.

Antibiotics Drugs like penicillin and sulphanomide which circulate in the bloodstream and prevent wounds from becoming infected.

Barrage A period of concentrated shelling by artillery.

Bayonet Knife-like weapon clipped on muzzle of rifle for close fighting; more often used for opening tin cans by most soldiers in World War II!

Bazooka Shoulder-fired rocket launcher for destroying tanks; all World War II armies had equivalents. Very conspicuous, and with a short effective range, they were efficient but dangerous to use.

Bunker Defensive position for infantry and/or heavy weapons, dug into ground and lined with concrete or timber.

Camouflage The art of hiding men or machines from enemy eyes by adopting colors and patterns which break up the outlines.

Campaign medal Medal given to a soldier not for an individual deed, but simply to mark that he served in a particular series of battles.

Carbine Short, light rifle, often used by people who needed to keep their hands relatively free, such as officers and vehicle crews.

Clip Slang for the magazine of a weapon; *or* the spring device holding enough cartridges for one loading of the magazine.

Company Small military unit of about five officers and 190 men at full strength.

Draft Term for conscription under the Selective Service Act.

Division Large military unit, with anything from 10,000 to 20,000 men depending upon number of regiments and other units assigned.

Engineers In military terms, specialist troops who took on such tasks as building, repairing, and running – or destroying – all kinds of camps, roads, railways, pipelines, fortifications, etc.

Field clothing Uniforms worn when actually fighting or training or doing dirty chores, rather than when turned out for parade.

Garrison cap Also called an overseas cap: a flat, limp cloth cap which can be slipped into the pocket or under the shoulder strap when not needed.

Hand grenade Small hand-thrown bomb, with enough explosive and steel splinters from the grooved casing to kill a bunched group of enemy soldiers.

Landing craft Simple barges used to transport soldiers from large ships to the landing beaches during amphibious operations. A ramp at the bow opened to let the men out; the flat bottom allowed the landing craft to come into shallow water.

Leave Also known as furlough – a short vacation when a soldier is allowed to return home to see his family.

Machine gun Weapon which fires rifle-size or larger bullets automatically, many times a second. The cartridges are fed in either from a belt or from a spring-loaded metal box (magazine) which clips on to the gun.

Timechart

Mess kit Soldier's equivalent of a plate and dish, for eating rations.

Mine Buried explosive charge, set off in various ways – pressure, tripwire, etc. – by men or machines passing over it.

Morphine Drug made from opium, used as a painkiller.

Mortar Simple smooth-barreled gun, used for lobbing small bombs at a high angle. A propeling charge in the base of the bomb is set off when it is dropped down the barrel on to a firing pin.

Platoon Small military unit of about 40 men led by a lieutenant or senior sergeant.

Poncho Waterproof sheet, used either as a rain cape or a groundsheet when camping.

Regiment Military unit made up of three battalions. A regiment contained about 2,500 men.

Replacement Newly trained soldier sent out to join a unit in battle, to take the place of a dead or wounded man.

Section Small military unit, usually of one NCO, a machine-gun crew, and six or seven riflemen, divided into two squads.

Signals In military terms, the troops who install and run the radio and field telephone network.

Sniper Expert marksman, usually equipped with telescopic sights, who lies in hiding to shoot unsuspecting enemies.

Spam Brand of processed, tinned meat eaten instead of fresh meat due to wartime shortages.

Suspenders The name for the shoulder harness straps of a soldier's webbing equipment, supporting the weight of the belt and the items fixed to it.

December 7, 1941 Japanese bomb US base at Pearl Harbor. Within days, USA at war with Japan and Germany and Japanese invade US-held Philippine Islands.

August 1942–January 1943 Grueling battle for Pacific island of Guadalcanal ends in US victory.

November 1942 US and Allied troops land in French North Africa, attacking Germans in Tunisia, who surrender in May.

June 1943 US landings on New Georgia, Solomon Islands, open amphibious campaign – landings on Japanese-held islands every few months from now on. Worst fighting on Tarawa (Nov. 1943), Peleliu (Sept. 1944), Philippines (Oct. 1944), Iwo Jima (Feb. 1945), Okinawa (April 1945).

July 1943 Allies land in Sicily.

September 1943 Allies land in Italy. Italians surrender, but occupying German armies fight on.

June 1944 Allies land in Normandy; and in Italy, reach Rome. Hard fighting in France, July–August, until large enemy forces trapped in "Falaise Pocket" and Allies race eastward, liberating Paris and Brussels. Allied landings in S. France.

December 1944–January 1945 Last German offensive in the West, the Battle of the Bulge in the Ardennes, is beaten off.

March 1945 US troops cross Rhine into Germany.

April 1945 US and Russian troops, advancing eastward and westward across Germany, meet at Elbe River.

May 1945 Germany surrenders to the Allied armies.

August 1945 Japan surrenders to the Allies after two atomic bombs are dropped at Hiroshima and Nagasaki.

Index